ACTIVE SERVICE

Copyright © Roy Summers/The Good Book Company 2008

Published by
The Good Book Company
Elm House, 37 Elm Road
New Malden, Surrey KT3 3HB, UK
Telephone 0845 225 0880; Fax: 0845 225 0990
email: admin@thegoodbook.co.uk
www.thegoodbook.co.uk

Except as may be permitted under the Copyright Act, no portion of this publication may be reproduced in any form or by any means without prior permission from the publisher.

ISBN 9781906334338
Cover design by Steve Devane
Printed in China

ACTIVE SERVICE

A GUIDE TO SERVING IN THE LOCAL CHURCH

ROY SUMMERS

WELCOME

Welcome to *Active Service!* A training course for all those involved in practical ministry in their local church.

Whether you are responsible for maintenance or money, flowers or food – this guide is designed to help you think through the biblical framework that undergirds your role. And to give you the opportunity to work out how you can do your job in the way that best glorifies God.

Throughout this training course, you will be referred to as a deacon. In some churches, the term deacon is used a great deal, in others it is barely mentioned at all. It is used here to refer to those who are actively serving in a specific, non-leadership role.

We will look at what the Bible says about deacons, and about serving the church in this role. The training guide is rooted in the Bible, because by it we may be 'equipped for every good work' (2 Timothy 3 v 17). 'Think Spots' will help you apply this to your own situation in more practical ways.

Active Service! is designed to be used in a small group. The studies could form the core of a training programme for people who are new to serving, but could equally be used to help refresh the more experienced. Alternatively, you can work through this guide on your own, or one-to-one with another Christian.

Roy Summers

CONTENTS

STUDY 1	WHAT IS A DEACON?	7
STUDY 2	A CRASH COURSE IN CHURCH GOVERNMENT	13
STUDY 3	WHAT MUST A DEACON BE?	21
STUDY 4	WHAT SHOULD A DEACON DO?	27
STUDY 5	HOW SHOULD A DEACON SERVE?	33
STUDY 6	RESPONSIBILITIES OF DEACONS	39
STUDY 7	MONEY MATTERS	45
STUDY 8	TESTING, TRAINING AND REVIEW	51
A FINAL WORD	THE FAITHFUL DEACON'S REWARD	57
APPENDIX 1	DEACONS' WIVES OR DEACONESSES?	59
APPENDIX 2	SAMPLE TASK DESCRIPTION	61

STUDY 1
WHAT IS A DEACON?

THIS STUDY TAKES A BROAD LOOK AT THE MINISTRY OF 'DEACONS' IN THE BIBLE.

MANY CHURCHES have officers called deacons – others have the role without using the word. The name itself comes from the Bible, but it is used in a range of ways in the pages of Scripture. This first study is an overview of what God's Word says about deacons, so that our understanding may be shaped by the Bible's teaching.

This first chapter focuses on what the Bible says about deacons; the next chapter will put this teaching into the context of church history, and how different churches are organised today.

STUDY 1

WHAT IS A DEACON?

It is significant that the Bible does not give a specific job description for deacons. We do however have three important clues:

CLUE 1: 'MINISTRY' = SERVICE

The English word *deacon* comes from a Greek word which is properly translated as the words ministry, minister, servant and service. The words related to 'deacon' appear about 100 times in the New Testament and cover a range of people serving within the church as well as outside it.

- The word for deacon/minister/servant may describe someone who washes feet (John 2 v 5, 9), or a government official (Romans 13 v 4), or the apostle Paul (Colossians 1 v 25; Philippians 1 v 1).
- The related words for ministry or service can describe the task of preaching the Word (Acts 6 v 4), or serving at tables (Luke 10 v 40) or the work of ministry in general (Ephesians 4 v 12, 1 Peter 4 v 10-11).

It is clear that the 'deacon' words of the New Testament are used to cover different activities, and most of the time the words are not used to describe someone who holds a particular office, or formal position in the church. But they *are* used to describe someone who serves, as this saying of Jesus makes clear (the 'deacon' words are highlighted in italics):

> Whoever would be great among you must be your *servant*, and whoever would be first among you must be your slave, even as the Son of Man came not to be *served* but to *serve*, and to give his life as a ransom for "many". (Matthew 20 v 26b-28)

● **THINK SPOT:**
1. What surprises you about this word study?

STUDY 1

2. What do we learn from it about a deacon's work?

CLUE 2: DIFFERENT QUALIFICATIONS

Two passages speak specifically about deacons who hold an office in the church. They are 1 Timothy 3 v 8-13 and Philippians 1 v 1. Acts 6 v 1-7 also mentions a form of ministry which is helpful in understanding the role of deacons. Deacons and elders have different ministries, and at this stage we want to note how the different ministries are indicated by the different qualifications required of them.

Read 1 Timothy 3 v 1-13

3. How many qualities are listed for elders? List them here:

4. How many for deacons? List them too:

5. How might you summarise the differences between them?

STUDY 1

6. How would the additional qualities specific to elders help them in their work of spiritual leadership and pastoral care?

7. What do we note about elders and deacons from Philippians 1 v 1?

The more extensive qualifications required of elders point to their role in teaching and pastoral care of the flock, a role not expected of deacons.

CLUE 3: PRACTICAL SERVICE NOT SPIRITUAL LEADERSHIP

The third main passage to consider is Acts 6 v 1-7. We will return to look at this passage in greater depth in Study 4, but for the moment we will take a brief look so as to grasp some general characteristics.

Read Acts 6 v 1-7

8. What was the difference between the service of the Seven and the service of the apostles?

9. Read Acts 20 v 28 and 1 Timothy 5 v 17 to see what the 'elders' are to do. What do Hebrews 13 v 17 and 1 Thessalonians 5 v 12-13 add about the work of the leaders of the congregation?

STUDY 1

The Seven served the church by practical care for the widows, so that the apostles could focus on the spiritual ministries of Word and prayer. In a similar way, the role of the deacon is to serve the church in practical ministries so that elders can focus on their calling to lead and care spiritually for the church.

> ● **THINK SPOT**
>
> *10. What sort of training will equip Christians for service as deacons? And what will support deacons as they serve the church in practical ways?*

> **SUMMARY**
>
> While the Bible does not give a specific 'job description' for the office of deacon, we have seen that deacons support the work of the elders in the local church. Elders are called to serve the congregation (including the deacons) through prayer and the ministry of the Word. Deacons are also to serve the congregation (including the elders) in a different way. The work of deacons is generally understood to be mainly practical in nature: certainly it is service, and it complements the elders' ministry of oversight, prayer and Word-ministry.
>
> In the next study we will see the different ways the role of church officers has been understood in the course of church history, and how it is often organised in churches today.

STUDY 2

A CRASH COURSE IN CHURCH GOVERNMENT

THIS STUDY LOOKS AT HOW THE ROLE OF DEACONS HAS BEEN UNDERSTOOD IN DIFFERENT TYPES OF CHURCH ORGANISATION.

A SURVEY of the Bible's teaching on 'deacons' gave us a broad description of the role, but no single blueprint for working out how deacons and elders relate to one another. There are several ways that Christians have tried to work out a biblical model for elders, deacons and the church. So how can elders and deacons work together in an effective way?

STUDY 2

CHURCH GOVERNMENT

These different ways of organising church life are called forms of church government, and we can group the common ones into four main types.

1. Episcopal (from the Greek for bishop/overseer)

Under this system, each local congregation is in the charge of a Vicar or Rector; a Bishop oversees a number of congregations (usually called a diocese). An Archbishop may oversee a number of dioceses. Within each local congregation there may be some lay church officers (Churchwardens) and a Church Council. Episcopal churches rarely have a permanent diaconate, and there is no common role for Deacons. The Church of England, for example, is episcopal. Confusingly, when ministers are ordained, they are usually ordained as a 'Deacon' and then a year later as a 'Priest'. These terms, however, are used in a very different way from the biblical usage we have been looking at.

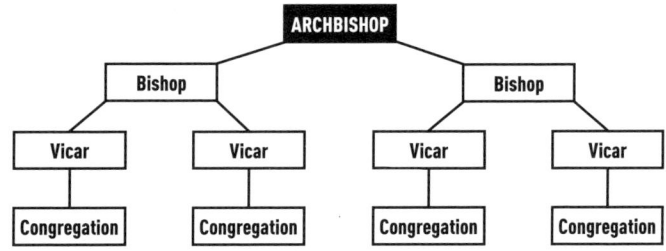

2. Presbyterian (from the Greek word for elder)

Each local congregation elects a 'Session' of Elders. The Pastor or Teaching Elder will be one of these Elders who together rule and care for the church.

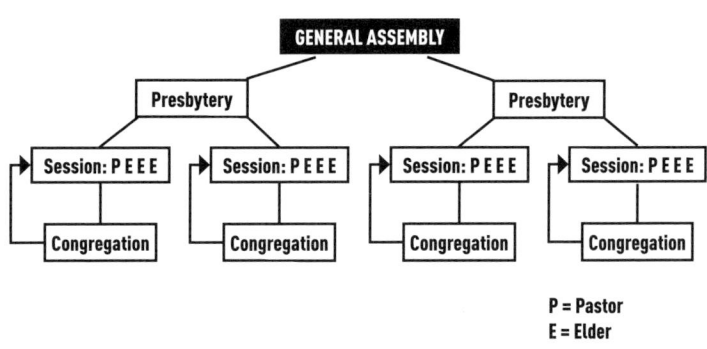

P = Pastor
E = Elder

STUDY 2

These Elders also belong to the 'Presbytery', a group of Elders which has oversight over several churches. There is a further level in that some members of the Presbytery are members of a 'General Assembly' which has final authority over all the churches.

Presbyterian church government is hierarchical, like the Episcopal system, but with the key difference that oversight is in the hands of a *group* of Elders, and that they are elected by the congregation.

There is usually no formal role for Deacons as church officers.

3. Congregational (from the view that authority rests with the congregation)

In this form of church government, decision-making is seen to be in the hands of the congregation, who will elect church officers. There is no single model for the relationship between Pastor, Elders, Deacons, Church Board (if there is one) and the congregation. The key distinctive is the role of the congregation in decisions. For more on this, see 'additional reading' at the end of the study.

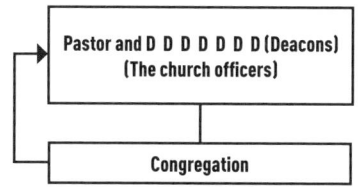

Other forms of congregational order

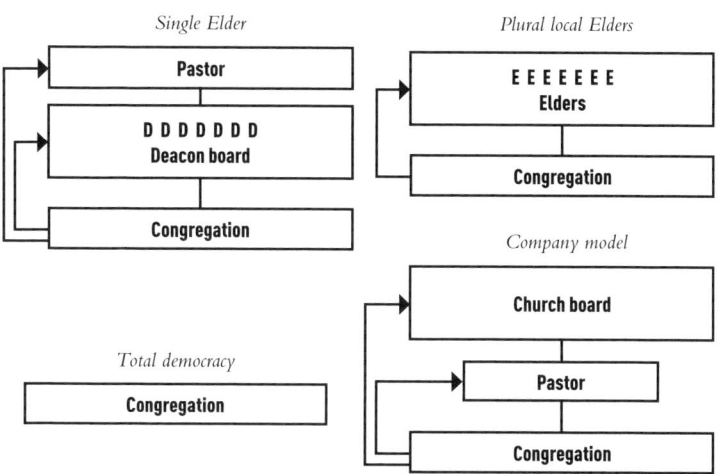

STUDY 2

4. Elder-Deacon

This is similar to the congregational model except, that decision-making and pastoral care lie with the Elders, while Deacons are responsible for practical support and service. Elders and Deacons together serve the congregation through their different ministries.

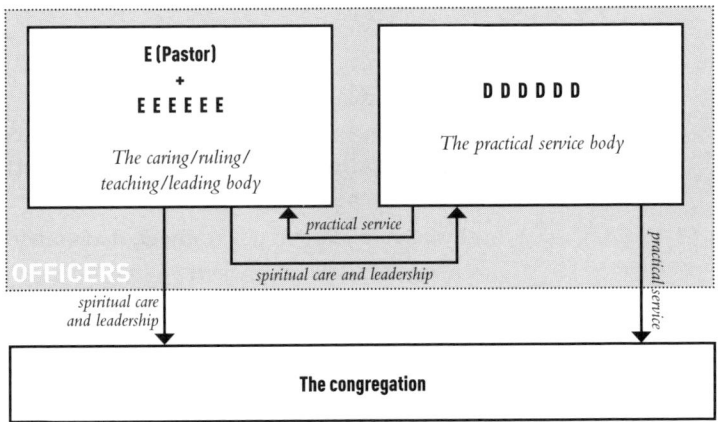

● THINK SPOT

1. Which forms of church government are you involved with? How do you relate to your leaders? And the congregation?

VITAL ASPECTS OF CHURCH GOVERNMENT

There is no single pattern for biblical church government, and each of the options we have just looked at has their strengths and weaknesses. We can, however, identify these vital aspects of the Bible's teaching on church order:

1. Jesus Christ is the sole head of the church

The Lord Jesus Christ not only died to redeem His people, but the

16

Bible clearly says that He is the head of the church. (see Ephesians 1 v 22-23, 4 v 15-16). We do not expect church government to be identical to the structures used in business and political bodies because the church is led primarily by Christ himself. And note, therefore, that any authority that a human leader has is a leadership that is in service of Christ. As Peter puts it, we are mere 'under-shepherds' to Jesus, who is the Chief Shepherd of God's flock (see 1 Peter 5 v 2-4).

2. The need for leadership
Leadership is a God-given gift and churches need to be led (Romans 12 v 8). Churches that do not allow this gift to be exercised are likely to lack focus, to have stunted growth and to miss the *dynamic* aspect of church life.

3. Two offices
Churches should have both elders and deacons. These two roles reflect the two kinds of service rendered in the church, that is, spiritual care and practical service (see 1 Peter 4 v 10-11): elders serve by spiritual care and deacons through practical service.

4. Several rather than a sole elder or deacon
There is wisdom in taking counsel with other mature believers, and we know that some congregations in the Bible had several elders and deacons (see Philippians 1 v 1; also Acts 6 v 2, 1 Tim 5 v 17). The congregation should also be involved in some way. This is often done by voting, but there are other (and maybe better) ways.

5. Flexibility
Churches should be dynamic organisms that have the ability to grow, change and plant new churches. There may be a need for different types of church government at different stages of life. A new church should probably not be tied down to one form of church government but be allowed to develop over time, and not to become rigid. For this reason it is generally unwise for a new church to adopt a fixed constitutional position on leadership in the church.

STUDY 2

● **THINK SPOT**

2. How are these vital aspects represented in your local church and its own form of church government?

3. Which form of organisation do you think works well, and which are not as strong?

LESSONS FROM CHURCH HISTORY

When we set the vital aspects of church government alongside the different models in existence today, we can make the following observations:

a) **Church government is an important but secondary doctrine.** It is important to have some kind of church government, but we should remember that it is the skeleton of church life and not the flesh. A body where the skeleton is always visible is not a pretty sight! Church government, like the bones, supports the church in the background. It is not to be the 'be all and end all' of church life.

b) **Different models of church government emphasise different aspects of church life.** For instance, the Episcopal model gives prominence to *the need for leadership*, which is also seen in the Presbyterian and to a lesser extent the Elder-Deacon systems. The gift of leadership can be completely lost in some congregational churches. The Presbyterian system gives prominence to *the benefit of having several elders*, which is hardly evident in Episcopal hierarchy. The congregational system by contrast gives prominence to *the involvement of the whole body* of believers (compare with Acts 6 v 2, 5-6).

c) **The need for two offices.** The strength of some forms of church government is the prominence they give to the distinct offices of elder (spiritual service) and deacon (practical service). We must remember that in the New Testament the words for 'elder' and 'deacon' (and for that matter 'overseer' or bishop) have quite broad meanings (see Study 1). The way we use and understand these terms within a specific form of church government may therefore be narrower than Scripture allows for.

d) **The place for change.** The church is a dynamic organism with has different needs at different times. A newly planted church may start with a single elder, and move towards a plurality.

● **THINK SPOT**
4. How has this study challenged your own thinking about how churches should be led and organised?

5. Now you understand your own church structure, how can you encourage better communication between yourself, the leaders and the congregation?

STUDY 2

> **SUMMARY**
> Each of the four main types of church government emphasise different biblical aspects of church life. In particular, their different understandings of the roles of elders and deacons should inform our own understanding of the deacon's ministry we serve in.

Additional Reading: *Systematic Theology*, Wayne Grudem (IVP), Chapter 47: Church Government.

STUDY 3

WHAT MUST A DEACON BE?

THIS STUDY TAKES A CLOSER LOOK AT THE PERSONAL QUALITIES OF DEACONS REQUIRED BY 1 TIMOTHY 3 v 8-13.

WE HAVE SEEN from Study 1 that deacons are people who serve, and from Study 2 that there are different forms this service may take, according to how our local church is organised. In this study, we take a closer look at one passage which lists the qualities required of a deacon. What you are called to be!

STUDY 3

● **THINK SPOT**

1. What behaviours and characteristics can prevent a deacon from serving effectively?

2. How would these affect the fellowship of the church?

The main passage dealing with deacons is 1 Timothy 3 v 8-13. (Verse 11 is dealt with separately below.) The most striking feature of these qualities is that they are more concerned with what a deacon *is* than what a deacon *does*.

Read 1 Timothy 3 v 8-10, 12-13

3. List the seven godly characteristics God expects deacons to maintain in their lives

The seven qualities Paul sets out divide well into three categories:

PERSONAL QUALITIES

1. **Dignified** or 'worthy of respect' (NIV). Someone who by virtue of character and example is naturally honoured by others.

2. **Not double-tongued** or 'not malicious talkers' (v 8). A straightforward character, not a deceiver, not two-faced in speech, nor a gossip, but an open and honest person.

STUDY 3

3. **Not addicted to much wine** or 'temperate' (verse 8). Someone who is known for their sobriety and seriousness; need not be teetotal, but must have no reputation, real or in jest, for drink.

4. **Not greedy for dishonest gain** (verse 8). A deacon may be asked to take responsibility for financial matters, and must be blameless in this area. They must not use their office for personal gain in any way.

● **THINK SPOT**

4. How do each of these qualities affect the way a deacon serves with:

Individuals?

Other deacons?

The elders?

The congregation as a whole?

SPIRITUAL QUALITIES

5. **Must hold the mystery of the faith with a clear conscience** or 'must keep hold of the deep truths of the faith with a clear conscience' (verse 9, NIV). Deacons must know the Christian faith well and live it for themselves. A clear conscience follows from the integrity of knowing the gospel and practising it in one's own life. Deacons must also have a clear conscience about being faithful to Christian teaching in the way they go about their responsibilities (see more in Study 7). A firm grasp of the gospel is therefore essential for godly practical ministry.

STUDY 3

MARRIAGE, FAMILY AND DOMESTIC QUALITIES

6. **The husband of one wife** (verse 12), does not mean that a deacon *must* be married, but refers to sexual purity whether married or not. And whether single or married, a deacon must not have a reputation as a flirt.

7. **Managing their children and their own households well** (verse 12). The word 'household' used here would have included wider responsibilities (servants etc.), so deacons must have their household and their wider affairs in good order. This demonstrates their suitability for service in the church, the household of God (see verse 5).

● **THINK SPOT**
5. *How will the absence or presence of these qualities affect a deacon's service in the church?*

QUALITIES FOR DEACONESSES

Verse 11 may refer either to female deacons (deaconesses) or to deacons' wives. If female deacons are in view (see Appendix 1) then they are to have the same character as deacons, with special attention to these characteristics:

8. **Dignified** or 'worthy of respect' (verse 11); as for deacons, she is to be the kind of woman that is naturally respected by those around her.

9. **Not slanderers** or 'malicious talkers' (verse 11), no reputation for gossip or damaging speech.

10. **Sober-minded** or 'temperate', i.e. level-headed and stable rather than up-and-down (the same word is found in 3 v 2).

11. **Faithful in all things** or 'trustworthy in everything' (verse 12); thoroughly reliable.

STUDY 3

● THINK SPOT

6. Why do you think these particular qualifications are given for deaconesses/wives of deacons?

7. What have you learnt from this study? Are you surprised that God is so concerned about your character when your job is essentially practical?

SUMMARY

God is more concerned with a deacon's character than with his gifts and deeds. In order to honour God with our work as deacons, we must never neglect these spiritual priorities. A further implication is that training and growth in godliness will equip us for better service as deacons.

STUDY 4
WHAT SHOULD A DEACON DO?

THIS STUDY DRAWS LESSONS FOR TODAY'S CHURCH FROM THE APPOINTMENT OF THE SEVEN IN ACTS 6 v 1-7.

IT'S VERY STRIKING that the list of qualities required of deacons in 1 Timothy 3 v 8-13 makes no reference to practical abilities. We are not told that 'a deacon must be good at task a, b or c', but that a deacon must have certain qualities of character. We see this emphasis in one passage (Acts 6 v 1-7) that describes the appointment of the Seven in the early church.

While the appointment of the Seven in Acts was in many ways a one-off, they are in some ways 'prototypes' of the office of deacon. We don't assume that because something happened in the early church we *must* do exactly the same; but we can see that their appointment enabled the apostles to focus on their ministry of Word and prayer, and that this helped the church to grow. That is a helpful pattern for elders and deacons today.

STUDY 4

Read Acts 6 v 1-7

1. What was the situation which required the appointment of these seven men?

2. What is surprising about the qualities these men must have?

3. What else did 'deacons' Stephen and Philip go on to do?
(Acts 6 v 8 – 7 v 53; 8 v 12, 26-40; 21 v 8)

4. What was the difference in role between the apostles and the Seven?

5. What light does this passage shed on the role of deacons?

Acts 6 gives us a snapshot in the life of the very early church. Seven men were appointed to take on a practical task delegated from the apostles, which otherwise threatened to hold the church back. As a result of their work, the Word of God continued to increase (v 7). Two of the men (Stephen and Philip) went on to exercise significant spiritual ministry in their own right. This passage describes what happened, and does not give us a once-for-all binding pattern for deacons in the church, but we can learn some principles from their experience.

STUDY 4

1. TEACHING AND PREACHING IS THE PRIORITY

The first principle is the **priority of the ministry of Word and prayer**. The apostles were becoming distracted from this ministry in order to care for the needy widows. When this responsibility had been delegated to others, the apostles continued with their ministry and the gospel began to spread again. This is one of a number of challenges to the church's growth overcome in Acts; see Acts 12 v 24 and 19 v 10.

2. DELEGATION IS VITAL

The second principle is that **delegating tasks enables the whole church to fulfil its purpose**. The apostles did not stop the church giving help to those in need in order to focus on their ministry of Word and prayer: they delegated this task to the Seven so that both spiritual ministry *and* the ministry of mercy could continue. In this way, delegating some tasks served the whole of the church's mission.

3. PRACTICAL TASKS ARE 'SPIRITUAL'

The third principle is that **delegated practical tasks are a ministry for which spiritual qualifications are needed**. Once again we note that spiritual qualities were asked for, and that the faithful exercise of the 'deacons' ministry enabled the spiritual work of the church to prosper.

Acts 6 never refers to the Seven as 'deacons' but the work of the seven helped the ministry of the apostles, and also served the whole congregation. Let's return to see how this works out in Acts 6.

Reads Acts 6 v 1-7 again

6. How did the 'deacons' serve the apostles? And how did they serve the congregation?

- *The seven men served* the congregation *by ...*

STUDY 4

- *The seven men served the apostles by...*

- *The seven men served the gospel by...*

WHAT RESPONSIBILITIES SHOULD DEACONS TAKE ON?

So what responsibilities should deacons take on in our churches? Out of all the practical ministries in a church, which ones should deacons take responsibility for? There is a danger that deacons take on too many practical ministries which rob the congregation of ways to serve. How do deacons decide which tasks to assume responsibility for? We pick up three clues from the experience of the Seven:

- The Seven took responsibility for *a task too big or too difficult for the congregation*. There was already a scheme for giving aid to poor widows (Acts 4 v 34-35). But with a growing church this became inefficient and was a cause of conflict (Acts 6 v 1). The congregation could no longer cope as things were, which is why someone had to take responsibility.

- The Seven took responsibility for *a task that would have hindered the duties of spiritual leadership*, namely the apostles' ministry of Word and prayer. The apostles *could* have coordinated the aid to Greek widows: indeed it is possible they were doing so up to this point. But now this had become a distraction to their spiritual leadership.

- The end result of the responsibilities that they took charge of was that the *overall spiritual work of the church was advanced*. Their service enabled the apostles to do their primary job without distraction.

STUDY 4

● **THINK SPOT**

7. *What are some of the real-life issues which have caused division or distraction in the life of a church you know? How did (or might) delegation help?*

THE PROTECTIVE ROLE OF DEACONS

When deacons serve well they protect the church:

1. **Deacons protect the church** by taking on responsibilities that may otherwise hinder the ministry and unity of the church. These tasks may be too big to go on without coordination, or too detailed to go before the whole-church meeting. It would be wrong for the church to become reliant on the deacons to do *all* the practical service in the church. But if someone has a practical need and knows no-one who can help them, then they should be able to turn to the deacons. Likewise if the spiritual leaders come across a practical need in the church they should be able to pass it to the deacons.

2. **Deacons protect the elders** by taking on responsibilities that would otherwise stop spiritual leaders from doing their job well. Practical tasks can be a distraction for elders as well as opening them up to unnecessary and trivial criticism. By taking on these responsibilities, deacons allow elders to give themselves to their ministry of Word and prayer.

SUMMARY

The Seven in Acts 6 were appointed to take on a practical ministry of mercy to the church widows in Jerusalem. Their experience suggests that deacons today can serve the whole church by taking on practical tasks that might be too big for the congregation or might distract the leaders from their spiritual ministries. In serving the church like this they also protect the church from unnecessary divisions.

STUDY 5
HOW SHOULD A DEACON SERVE?

THIS STUDY IS ABOUT THE WAY DEACONS SERVE CHRIST, AND THE WAY THEY RELATE TO ONE ANOTHER AND TO OTHER CHURCH OFFICERS.

BECAUSE DEACONS are engaged in a spiritual ministry, *how* we serve matters a great deal. We need to cultivate a godly attitude towards any service we perform for others.

STUDY 5

A SPIRITUAL ATTITUDE

● THINK SPOT

1. How might you respond to the following situations?
   How would a **spiritual** response differ from a **worldly** response?

- Someone needs a lift to a meeting, and there is no-one else who could give it?

- You feel too tired to do your regular job at church?

- No-one thanks you for what you do in the church?

The right attitude, which in the end is a reflection of the heart, is vital. We can spoil our service if we do it in the wrong spirit. Our attitude must reflect the character of Christ.

● THINK SPOT

2. What might be the signs that we are serving with wrong and right attitudes?

Signs of serving with...	...a right attitude	...a wrong attitude
Out of love Galatians 5 v 13		

STUDY 5

Signs of serving with...	...a right attitude	...a wrong attitude
Without complaining Philippians 2 v 14		
Humbly Matthew 20 v 26-28		

We also need to be flexible and teachable. Have you heard this joke about deacons?

Q: 'How many deacons does it take to change a light bulb?'
A: 'What? *Change*?!'

We can become inflexible if we are too possessive of our area of service and unwilling to have things changed. We think this way if we have a wrong view of our role: a deacon is a servant of the church and its leaders. In these and many other ways we need to nurture spiritual attitudes in service.

IN SPIRITUAL PARTNERSHIP

In 1 Timothy 3 v 1-13 and Philippians 1 v 1 deacons and elders are mentioned together. In Acts 6 v 1-7 the seven 'deacons' were appointed to help the apostles. These examples show that deacons work as a team and in partnership with the other office-holders of the church (however it may be organised).

First, deacons must relate well together as a team. This means we need to meet and pray together regularly. Social gatherings and informal meals help to build good relationships, and consulting other deacons is wise (Proverbs 13 v 10). Here are some things that can harm relationships between deacons:

- One deacon is not pulling their weight through laziness, or because they are overworked in other areas of life and need a break.
- A deacon is domineering – perhaps through pride or through being in the role for too long!

- Someone guards their 'patch' jealously and is secretive about their work.
- One deacon resents another in an 'easier' work/family situation who seems unwilling to help with certain tasks.
- Poor communication and imprecise boundaries between responsibilities leading to tension.

Secondly, deacons must also relate to the eldership of the church, who bear final responsibility (1 Timothy 5 v 17). Some types of service have leadership and pastoral implications, and deacons should be sure to run their plans for these kinds of task past the church leadership (see further Study 6).

Finally, deacons must work at relationships within the whole church family. This is true of every church member, of course (Colossians 3 v 12-14), but if a relationship is drifting, or has gone wrong, then those in active service must be exemplary in being quick to correct it. Disagreements between deacons and others in the church may cause a division that affects the whole body.

THE SUPPORT OF THE DEACON'S FAMILY

A deacon's duties at church must not lead him (or her) to neglect their responsibilities at home. We saw earlier from 1 Timothy 3 v 12 that they must manage their own households well; deacons' spouses are inevitably involved and should be supportive. Whether verse 11 refers to deacons' wives or to female deacons (see Appendix 1), the home remains a prior responsibility. Deacons who cannot combine church and home responsibilities should consider stepping back in order to give proper time at home, their first priority.

● THINK SPOT
3. What can you do to foster teamwork and partnership between the different groups serving in church life?

STUDY 5

4. How might you organise meetings to build good relationships with one another and with the elders?

5. What is the place of praying together in deacons' meetings?

6. What communication to and from other groups in church (e.g. the elders) will help you to undertake your duties in partnership *and* with a godly attitude?

7. What else would you like to see change in church? How will you take this matter up?

SUMMARY

The deacon's attitude before God and in service is vital to a godly and effective ministry. Deacons also work in partnership with other deacons, and with other church officers. We need to give attention to these relationships, bear in mind the pastoral implications of our duties, and work to serve the whole church and not our own interests.

STUDY 6
RESPONSIBILITIES OF DEACONS

IN THIS STUDY WE TURN TO SOME VERY PRACTICAL ASPECTS OF HOW DEACONS CARRY OUT THEIR RESPONSIBILITIES.

THE RESPONSIBILITIES OF DEACONS will vary from church to church. They will also change over time as church life develops. For this reason we will only be able to generalise here because your situation is bound to be unique. The biblical guidelines are clear: deacons are to serve the church and elders in practical ways.

While deacons have the responsibility that practical care is carried out, it does not mean they personally must do it all. Indeed, deacons may serve the church better by leading a team of volunteers involved in a particular area.

STUDY 6

TYPICAL AREAS OF RESPONSIBILITY

We could group general duties under these headings:

Practical care of people
- Money problems
- Housing/transport/other needs
- Visitation (i.e. visiting church members)

Practical care of elders
- Ensuring elders are able to do their work of prayer and ministry of the Word effectively.
- Ensure they are not burdened with practical responsibilities.

Practical matters in meetings of the church
- Setting up
- Temperature
- Safety
- Door welcoming
- PA/ sound system, recording sermons.

Management and care of material
- Finance
- Property

Church administration
- Bookings and diaries
- Office administration

● **THINK SPOT**

1. Can you think of any additional practical responsibilities in your fellowship that should fall to deacons (see 'The Protective Role of Deacons' in Study 4)?

2. Any that might fall *either* to deacons *or* to elders?

STUDY 6

A CHECKLIST FOR ORGANISING SPECIFIC TASKS

If you are given a specific task, this checklist will help you make sure that you are able to do it effectively.

- [ ] Discuss the task with other deacon(s) and elders.
- [ ] Know who is responsible for what task and draw up Specific Task Guidelines (see next section).
- [ ] Ensure that all deacons know something about each role.
- [ ] When the task is given to someone in the church, it is vital that they are given clear instructions and then periodic feedback.
- [ ] Consider the pastoral implications of the role: how does a job well done serve the gospel, the church, and the elders?

One common way to delegate tasks is by forming a rota. While these can be a convenient way to organise responsibilities, there are some disadvantages:

> ● **THINK SPOT**
> *3. What are the benefits of rotas? Any disadvantages?*
>
>
>
> *4. What are the effects of rotas on :*
> *(a) a sense of teamwork,*
>
>
> *(b) taking responsibility?*
>
>
>
> *5. Who should draw up rotas?*

STUDY 6

SPECIFIC TASK GUIDELINES

When a specific task is given to an individual, it's helpful to be clear about what the role requires and what is involved. One way to do this is to draw up some Specific Guidelines, or a Task Description. This could list the duties and give:

    a)   Task Name
    b)   Short Description of the task
    c)   Gifts or experience that would be helpful
    d)   Eldership/pastoral implications

● **THINK SPOT**
Write down some guidelines for the following tasks:

a) Church Address List
b)

c)

d)

a) Care of the Elderly and Infirm
b)

c)

d)

STUDY 6

a) Administration of Help to the Poor
b)

c)

d)

a) Door Stewarding
b)

c)

d)

An example can be found in Appendix 2

COMMUNICATION

Church members need to know who they can turn to for help, so it is important to make a list of the elders' and deacons' responsibilities available. This could be drawn up at least annually and each member given a copy. It could form part of a church prayer diary as well—if these tasks are recognised as spiritual, then we should all be praying that they are done well!

SUMMARY
Clear guidelines and good communication are essential. Regular reviews for those in post are also useful and will be covered in Study 8.

STUDY 7
MONEY MATTERS

THIS UNIT GIVES AN OVERVIEW OF BIBLICAL TEACHING ABOUT MONEY TO EQUIP THOSE WHO DEAL WITH FINANCE.

WE SAW IN STUDY 3 ('Spiritual Qualities') that deacons must have a clear conscience about obeying biblical teaching in the way they go about their responsibilities. As finance is often a specific responsibility of deacons, it is useful to have an overview of the Bible's teaching to help us discharge these duties well.

STUDY 7

RESPONSIBILITY FOR FINANCE POLICY AND MANAGEMENT

Elders have oversight of, and direct the affairs of, the church, and this should include the financial policy. Specific aspects of *carrying out* this policy may lie with the deacons. Biblical teaching doesn't always divide responsibilities quite this neatly, so what follows may touch on both areas. In finance as in any other area, deacons should consult elders where their work may have pastoral implications.

Money is an important area of teaching, and we cannot hope to cover everything here. Money itself is not evil: it is the *love* of money that is a root of all kinds of evil (1 Timothy 6 v 10). We need to be well-taught in this area so that we are wise in our use of money for the sake of the gospel.

We will look briefly at principles governing advice on giving, handling church finances, the support of church workers and the support of poor believers.

PRINCIPLES FOR ADVICE ON GIVING

Church members may ask deacons for advice on giving. Paul's second letter to the Corinthians encourages us to give:

- **Generously** because God is no man's debtor and we will find a great blessing in giving (2 Corinthians 9 v 6). We should also give **cheerfully**, and not reluctantly or under compulsion (v 7).
- **According to our means** (2 Corinthians 8 v 11). Old Testament believers gave one tenth of their wealth to the temple and some Christians take this to be a helpful guideline for today.
- **Regularly** or at least in a planned way, so that our actual giving matches our willingness to give (2 Corinthians 8 v 11).

If you do not already hav one, it is good for your church to prepare a booklet on giving, explaining the church budget, gift aid and standing-order forms, including a brief summary of the Bible's teaching, so that members can be informed.

PRINCIPLES FOR HANDLING CHURCH FINANCES

Deacons may be involved in collecting and spending money on behalf of the church. As this money is being held in trust for the church, it must be handled in a transparently honest way. Good practice also reduces the opportunity for greed and fraud. Basic wisdom suggests that:

- More than one person should be involved in the finances of the church so that finances are *seen* to be handled correctly. When Paul sent a collection for the relief of the poorer Christians, he sent at least two brothers to accompany the money. (2 Corinthians 8 v 16 – 9 v 5). In a similar way, we should not be alone to count collections and other sums of money;
- There should be appropriate controls on expenditure: spending should be according to agreed priorities, from agreed budgets, and may require approval and/or a counter-signature. Regular accounts should be available to the church leadership so that all is done in good order.

More broadly, the Bible teaches us to pay what we owe (Romans 13 v 8), not to hoard money for ourselves, and to be prudent. These will inform the overall financial policy (which we have seen is normally the responsibility of elders), but may well affect the way deacons carry out their own role.

● **THINK SPOT**

1. What principles do you think govern the way money is spent in your church?

2. What are the striking differences between your church's approach to money, and running a business?

STUDY 7

Two particular areas of expenditure that may be administered by deacons are the support of gospel workers, and the support of poor believers.

THE SUPPORT OF GOSPEL WORKERS

The local church has an obligation to support gospel workers: first the local workers (including the pastor) and then gospel partners working elsewhere.

Pastors and full-time gospel workers are entitled to be supported by the church for their work (1 Corinthians 9 v 14; Galatians 6 v 6 and 1 Timothy 5 v 18). They should be paid so they can get on with the work unhindered, and honoured for their work through their wage (see 1 Timothy 5 v 17-18: a muzzled ox couldn't be expected to perform well).

Gospel workers should not however be a *burden* to the church, and may need to take responsibility for providing for themselves if the church is not able to support them fully.

A gospel worker may for missionary reasons choose not to ask for support from those they are working among, but that decision belongs to the worker rather than the church. The apostle Paul gave up this right in order not to be a burden on those he was trying to reach (see 1 Thessalonians 2 v 9). In some cases, Paul was supported by his own labour (as in Thessalonica), in others by gifts from churches in *partnership* (Philippians 4 v 14-16).

In our support of gospel workers at home and away we should honour our obligations to them and to the ministry by providing adequately and cheerfully, so that they can continue to work wholeheartedly for our benefit.

THE SUPPORT OF POOR CHRISTIANS

A second obligation on Christians is to support those who are in need. As the local church is God's household, we have responsibilities to one another if our brother or sister is in need. We are not to support those who are lazy (2 Thessalonians 3 v 10), nor those whose believing family are able to meet the need (1 Timothy 5 v 3-4). The very strict criteria of 1 Timothy 5 are there to protect the church from unscrupulous people who may see the church as a 'soft touch'.

It makes sense for the church to agree some basic guidelines, to help deacons assess whether the need is genuine and whether it is,

STUDY 7

appropriate for the church rather than relatives, say, to provide the help.

Sometimes the greatest need will be sound advice on managing money. There is room for grace here: some sort of financial assistance (e.g. a loan) while they are getting out of a financial mess may be appropriate, even if not strictly deserved according to the criteria set by the church.

● **THINK SPOT**

3. What are the guidelines in your church for giving help to needy believers?

4. What attitudes sometimes hold us back from being generous in this area?

STUDY 8
TESTING, TRAINING AND REVIEW

THIS FINAL STUDY SUGGESTS A PROCEDURE FOR TRAINING, SELECTING AND SUPPORTING DEACONS.

OUR STUDIES in this Guide have been rooted in the Bible because the Scriptures contain everything we need for *training* (2 Timothy 3 v 16-17):

All Scripture is breathed out by God and profitable for teaching, for reproof, for correction, and for training in righteousness, that the man of God may be competent, equipped for every good work.

STUDY 8

TRAINING AND TESTING

The Bible assumes we will be trained and so we need to be teachable as deacons. Training as a deacon can take time, and indeed continues all the way through our service. We should expect everyone who serves in the church to undergo training. This will equip us with our specific role, and help to keep our attitude godly.

The Scriptures also require that a (potential) deacon be shown to be suitable by practical experience.

> **Read 1 Timothy 3 v 10**
> *1. Why must deacons be tested?*

We should therefore expect a period of 'probation' and training *before* we are formally recognised as a deacon by the church. It may be that during this time we discover we are not cut out for the role of deacon: we must still serve Christ, but in another capacity.

If we put these teachings into practice, our procedure for training deacons may look like this:

1. Identify candidates with the right qualities

Candidates are chosen because they have the right *character*. See Study 3 for more detail on these qualities. The period of training and testing will show whether these people are right for the role, but the first step is to look for a godly character.

2. Training period

During this time, potential or 'trainee' deacons have opportunity to learn the role of deacon and take responsibility together. They also undergo training for the role (Studies 1-7) and have periodic one-to-one reviews. This period provides the 'testing' of deacons mentioned above.

3. Church confirmation

The church may comment in confidence, move to confirm the status as deacon, and recognise this in some way (a vote or act of commissioning).

STUDY 8

4. Periodic review

Deacons continue to receive training and be reviewed because their work matters to the church. One way to do this is described in 'Review Process' below.

> ● **THINK SPOT**
>
> 2. Why should we train and test potential deacons?
>
>
> 3. How does a church demonstrate that a ministry is valuable? Does this happen in your church?

VISION AND VALUES

As church officers, deacons should understand the life of their local church and be comfortable with the church's values and emphases. Part of the training and testing process should be to explore this area. Some churches will have a formal statement of beliefs, church principles and vision statement. Others will have a way of operating that is known but not spelled out in writing.

As servants of the whole church we need to be familiar with these values so that our work – however detailed – can contribute to the big picture of church life.

> ● **THINK SPOT**
>
> 4. Vision: Does your church have a vision statement or mission statement? If not, how would you describe your church's aims?

STUDY 8

5. Values: Which aspects of the Christian life are most clearly emphasised in your church?

6. How do you feel about these answers?

REVIEW PROCESS

Regular reviews show that what we do is significant. Most leadership teams will review the church's programmes, special events and regular activities because these are important enough to be done well. And if we think something is no longer working well, then review is an opportunity to change.

Because the deacon's ministry matters, it is important to review it, probably annually. The heart of a review process is the discussion that takes place, rather than the 'result' of answering certain questions.

We should make sure that our review discussion covers at least these four areas:

- **Does my performance need to change?** There *is* a place for loving confrontation if change is needed. It may be that a *way of doing things* needs to change rather than our individual performance. Review is a time to talk about this.
- **Have I or my situation changed?** As people and as Christians we grow and change. As we put one set of God-given gifts to use, others may emerge. If we think of the Seven in Acts 6 v 1-7, we recall that Stephen and Philip went on to have significant ministries as evangelists (see Study 4). Review is a time to talk about 'where next'?
  A second area of change is that our personal circumstances may mean we are no longer able to serve as before if we have extra family responsibilities, or additional health concerns, for example.

A third area might be that, having mastered our current responsibilities, we have room to take on some more!
- **Has the role or has the church changed?** Too often we assume that deacons' roles and responsibilities carry on unchanged. If, as we would hope, the shape of church life changes as God brings new people and new opportunities, then we should expect the roles of the deacons to change. Review is a time to talk about this.
- **Are the right relationships in place?** Do we have the right level of support and communication from those we report to (eldership for instance)? Are we meeting and working as a team, and giving ourselves to partnership and teamwork (Study 5)?

SUMMARY

The ministry of deacons is important.

As a church, we show that deacons matter by making sure that the right people are chosen for this ministry, that they are trained and tested according to biblical criteria, and that they receive support in their work.

As deacons, we demonstrate the value of ministry by being teachable and submitting to the church's discernment of our best areas of service. We can also use regular reviews to hear as well, as to suggest, how our ministry can serve the church better.

A FINAL WORD
THE FAITHFUL DEACON'S REWARD

GODLY DEACONS ARE A BLESSING to any local church. Our prayer has been that *Active Service* has helped you and your fellow deacons to be equipped to serve the local church as a deacon.

We have seen that deacons' roles come in different shapes and sizes, according to the particular model of your church. We have also seen that the Bible has more to say about what kind of person a deacon is to *be* than about what they are to *do*. As deacons, we are to work together with one another, in partnership with the elders, and for the benefit of the whole church.

Serving others can be hard, especially if we are busy and people seem ungrateful. Let us finish with this encouraging verse from the end of our main passage about deacons (1 Timothy 3 v 13):

> *For those who serve well as deacons gain a good standing for themselves and also great confidence in the faith that is in Christ Jesus.*

What a great encouragement!

APPENDIX 1

DEACONS' WIVES OR DEACONESSES?

1 Timothy chapter 3 begins by listing the qualities needed in an elder. At verse 8, Paul moves on to describe the required qualities for a deacon. The verse says, 'Deacons likewise…' because in the same way that elders must have certain qualities, so must deacons.

Verse 11 begins in the same way as verse 8 with a 'likewise' to show there is a connection between the deacons being described in v 8-10 and the women described in verse 11. The question is who these women are:

Some suggest that Paul has in mind the wives of deacons. But nothing is said to the wives of elders in verses 1-7. And we expect the 'likewise' of verse 11 to introduce a new group, as it did in verse 8.

A better suggestion is that Paul refers to the office of deaconess or female deacon, because they are mentioned as another group alongside the deacons. The word can mean either 'women' or 'wives' (NIV has added 'their wives'). And Romans 16 v 1 tells us of Phoebe a servant (literally 'deacon') of the church, suggesting there were women deacons elsewhere.

It seems more likely therefore that Paul is referring to the office of deaconess or female deacon.

APPENDIX 2

SAMPLE TASK DESCRIPTION

a) Task Name: **Door Steward**
b) Short Description: **Welcome people to the meeting and ensure they receive any handouts.**
c) Gifts/experience helpful: **Reliability, friendliness**
d) Eldership/Pastoral Implications: **Chosen with advice of leaders**

The noble task of Door Steward
The door steward is often the first person to greet a worshipper. Regulars, especially if they are finding life hard, will benefit from a warm bright welcome in Christ's name. Visitors, especially, need a friendly face and a helping hand. This is a vital part of their welcome.

The duties of the Door Steward
- Arrive early to ensure everything is in place: entrance area clean, books and sheets available to be handed out.
- Welcome people with a bright smile and give them relevant materials. Newcomers may need to be told about Sunday School or Crèche arrangements, where they can hang their coats, and where the toilets are.
- At the start of the meeting, ensure that people don't walk into the meeting during prayers/readings etc.
- After the meeting, see that everything is put back – but not so quickly that the congregation is made to feel uncomfortable!

NOTES

NOTES

LEARN2LEAD

Learn2Lead is a training course based in local churches to prepare people for leadership in the church. It aims to equip members of the congregation with the skills they need to move into leadership.
- Ready-made training package with tutor support available
- Bible-centred throughout
- Tried, tested and refined over many years
- Trains students in vital areas of ministry

Who is it for?
Any leader or potential leader, perhaps someone who will become a leader in the next few years, including:

- Home group leader
- Youth leader
- Sunday School leader
- Elder
- Deacon
- Specialist group leader (women's group, old people, students)

How does it work?
Learn2Lead has five tracks.
1. Understanding the Bible,
2. Understanding Doctrine,
3. Understanding Leadership,
4. Leadership in Practice 1
5. Leadership in Practice 2

Each track has 10 units, with leader's notes contained in the comprehensive Tutor Manual.

There are three ways of using **Learn2Lead**:
1. **Two-year leadership programme** – a group meets regularly with a tutor (often a pastor) to work through all five tracks.
2. **Pick and mix** – = pick whichever track suits your needs or the needs of your congregation.
3. **Individual study** – individuals can choose to work through tracks on their own.

For more information and to order contact
The Good Book Company **on 0845 225 0880**
or visit www.thegoodbook.co.uk